New Seasons is a registered trademark of Publications International, Ltd.

© 2006 New Seasons®
All rights reserved.
This publication may not be reproduced in whole or in part by any means
whatsoever without written permission from:

Louis Weber, CEO
Publications International, Ltd.
7373 North Cicero Avenue
Lincolnwood, Illinois 60712

www.pilbooks.com

Permission is never granted for commercial purposes.

Manufactured in China.

8 7 6 5 4 3 2 1

ISBN 10: 1-4127-5494-1
ISBN 13: 978-1-4127-5494-1

REAL *Sisters* NEVER GROW UP

Written by V.C. Graham

new seasons®

Hi, I'm Sarah. I'll be the one who really raises you.
Those other two are only here to drive us around for 16 years.

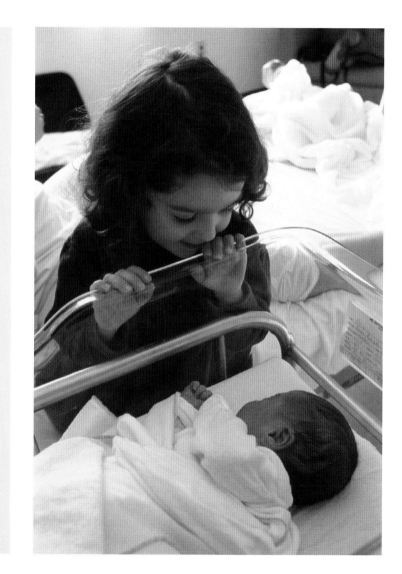

Careful.

Mommy said she swallowed a watermelon seed,
and that's how come her tummy got so big
with you in it.

Mommy and Daddy said I should
ask you to bring us a baby sister.

But between you and me,
I think they'd rather have a pony.

Ever wonder why Mom always
called us Thelma and Louise?

Remember when "Dare-ya" was our middle name?

I think we made a wrong turn
at the tan, glistening, shirtless
farmer driving the tractor.

We should turn around and go back.

Gossip between sisters is not gossip at all.

It is a frank discussion of
social affairs and cultural behavior.

We're not afraid to get a little gritty.

We're not competitive.
We just want to win.

You understand that it isn't
about the size of the diamond,
but the size of his heart.

We're calling from the library
to let you know we'll be home a little late.

Hi, Dad!
We're calling from the library again!

Sometimes it's okay to have a pushy sister.

Remember playing Spring Break?
After we finished our pretend beers,
we jumped into the pretend pool,
and pretended to take our tops off. . .

And when we're asleep, our dolls come alive. . .

No, dear. I'm afraid we can't
trade her in for a quieter one.

Bad to the bone.

Let's go over the plan again.

I say I have a headache and go to bed.

You turn up the TV so they
can't hear my window open.

Listen up, baby sister—
this is the only time it's okay to be fast.

At least we can truthfully say that
our first set of wheels was a two-seater convertible!

Exactly where did you think
I could wear this again?

I didn't really mind sharing a bath with you.
At least you kept the water warm.

If we had to inherit one thing from Mom,
at least it was her fine . . .

taste in swimwear.

Tell you what: I'll have mine tattooed,
so we don't get them mixed up again.

Yeah, we've still got 'em.

Don't tell anyone, but the bumpy part of the road
actually feels really interesting.

It's okay. I can always cut them out of your hair later.

One minute you were a sister,
and the next minute you were a princess.

I don't really care who called the police—
it got us out of practicing piano for a while.

Let's do take it with us!

I couldn't decide which ones to buy.

Then I remembered what you always say:
Buy them all.

I don't think anyone suspects
we're sisters, do you?

No matter what happened in school that day,
we were always laughing by the time we got home.

Sometimes it's hard to remember
where I end and you begin.

Real sisters can have an entire conversation
without speaking a word.

No amount of formal training
can prepare you for being a sister.

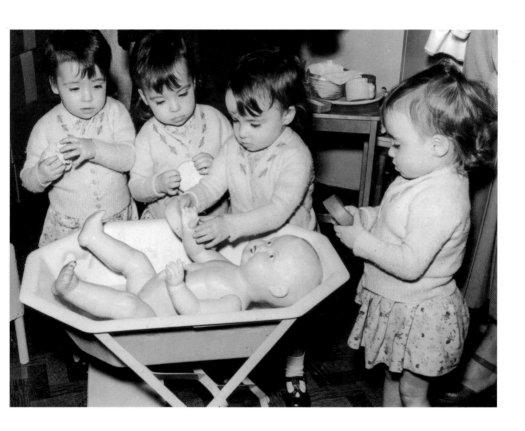